The Worst FUCK OFF

Phenomenal Swear Word To Color For Stress Releasing

C.J. Willoughby

Happy Coloring!

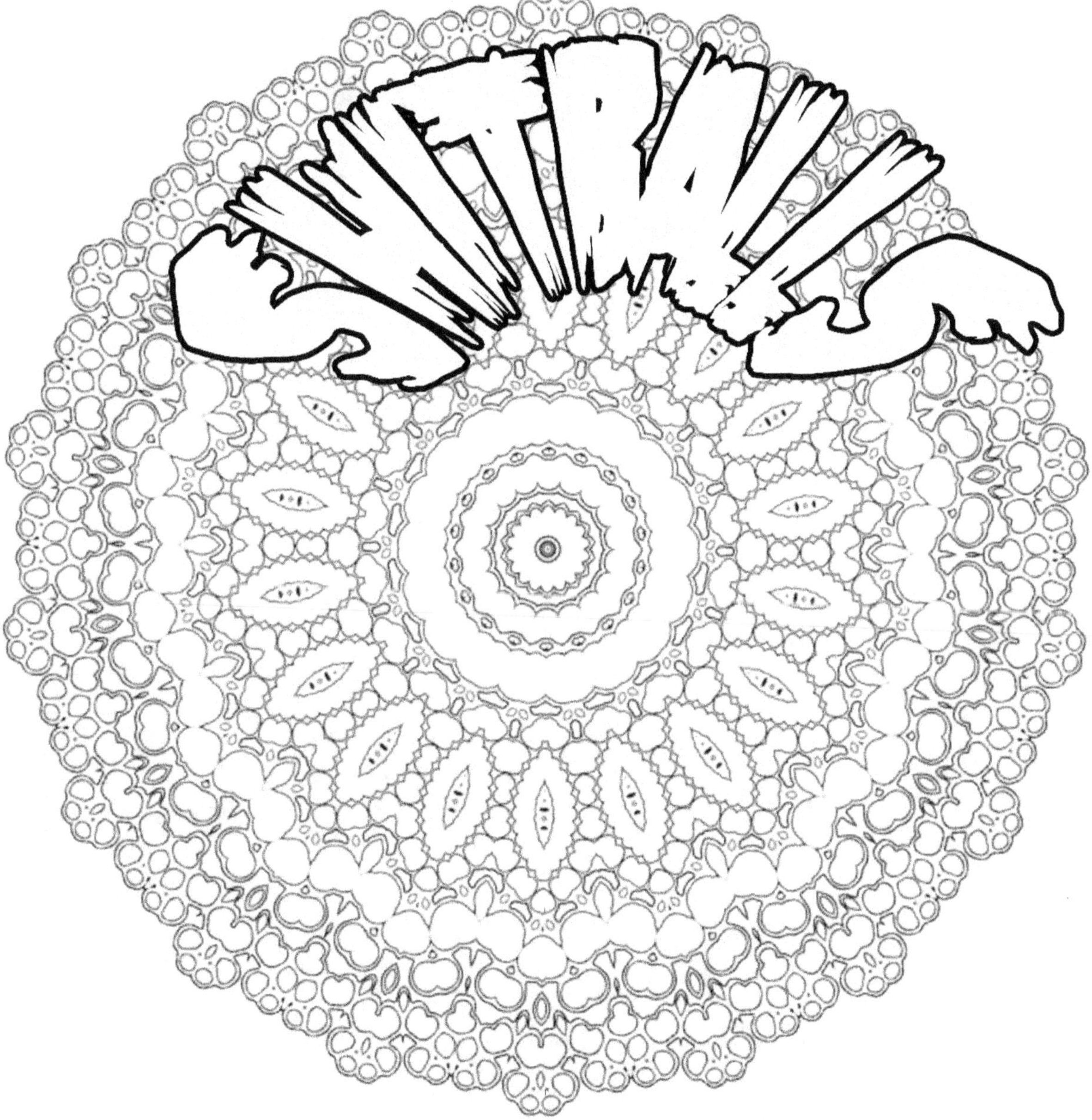

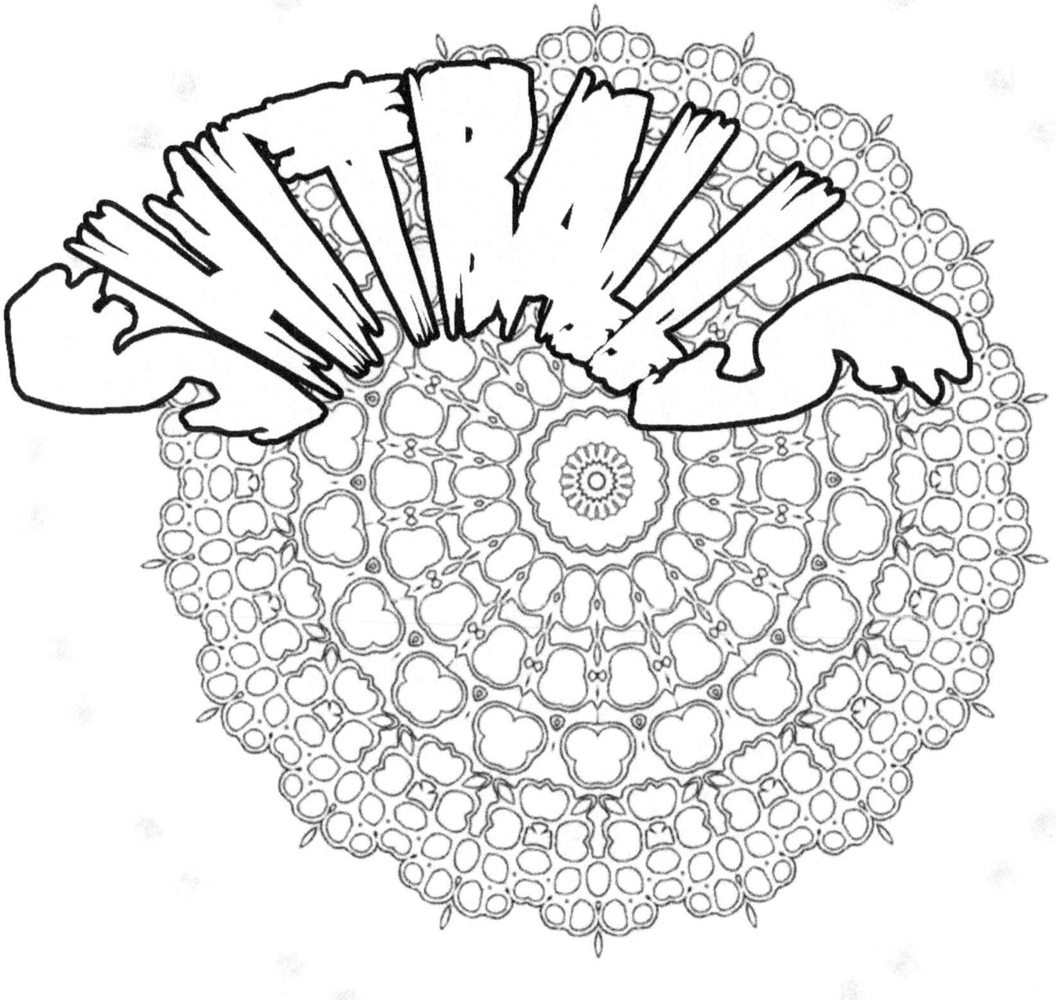

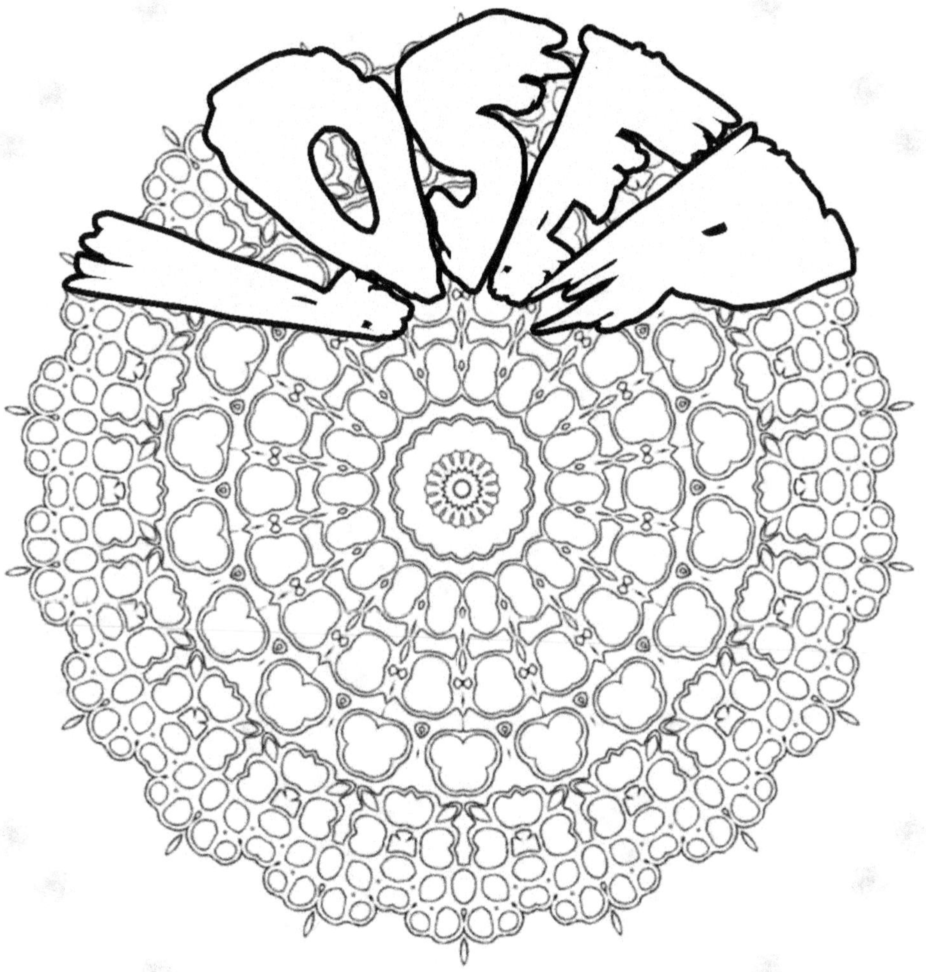

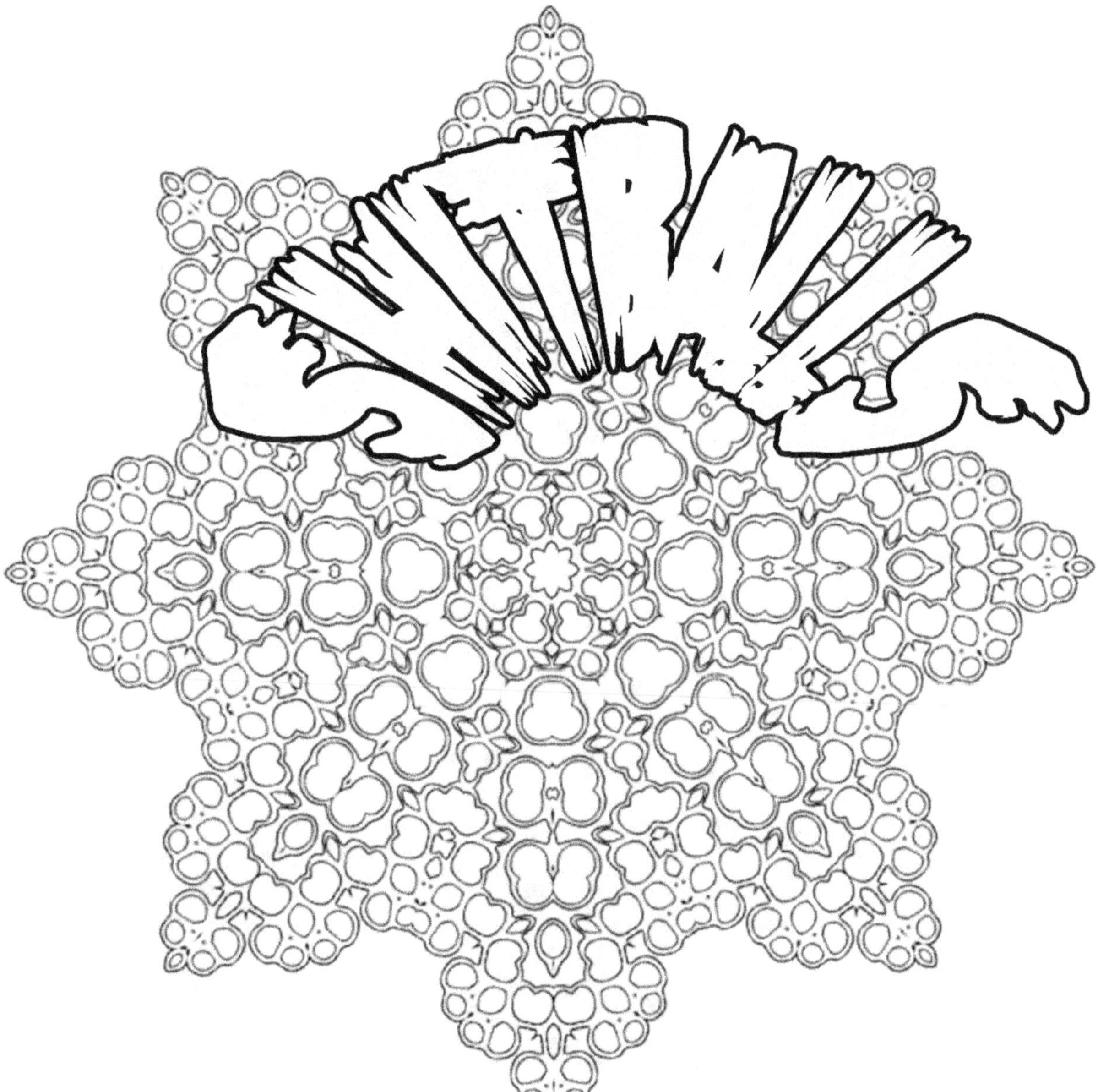

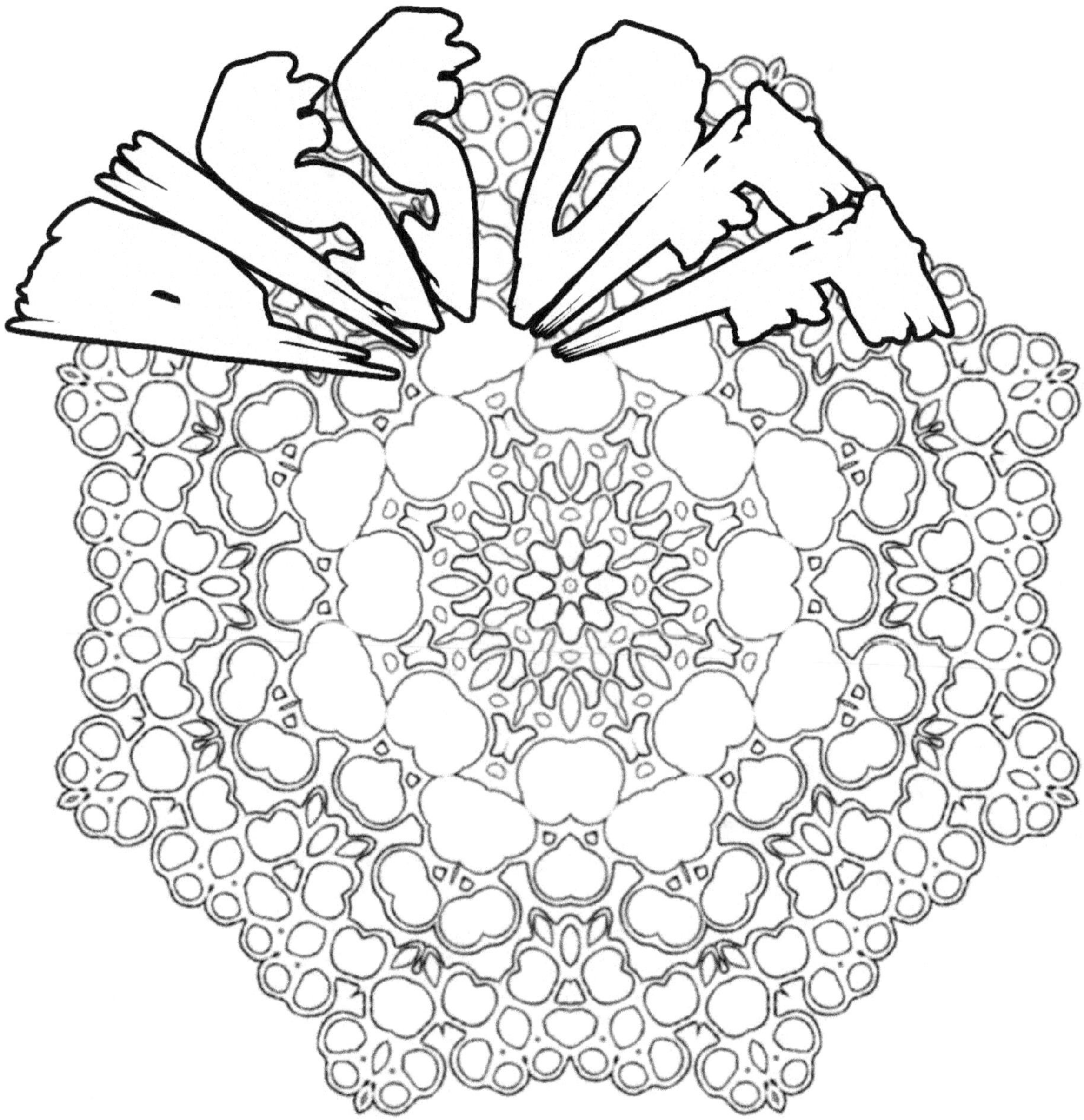

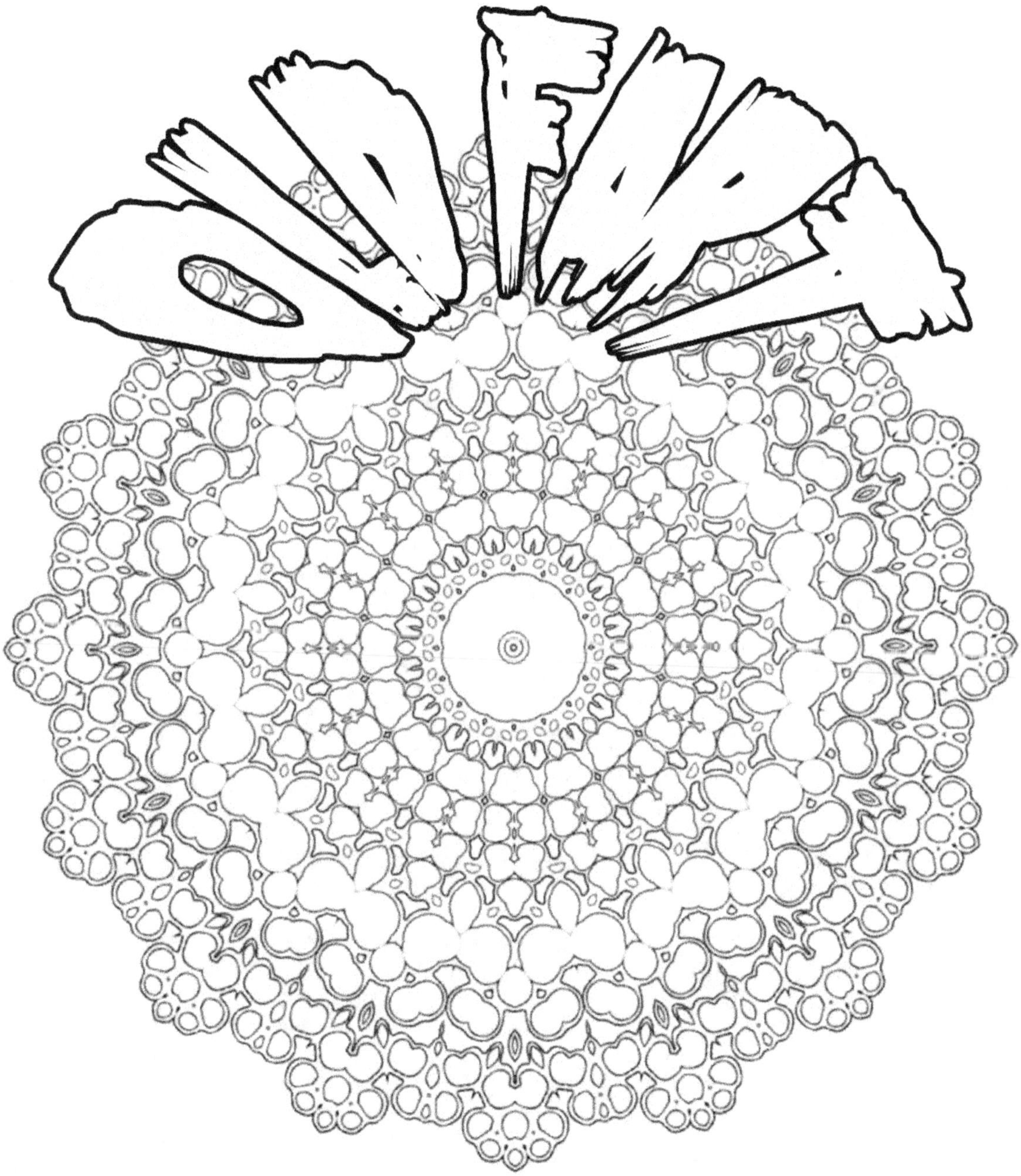
OLD FART

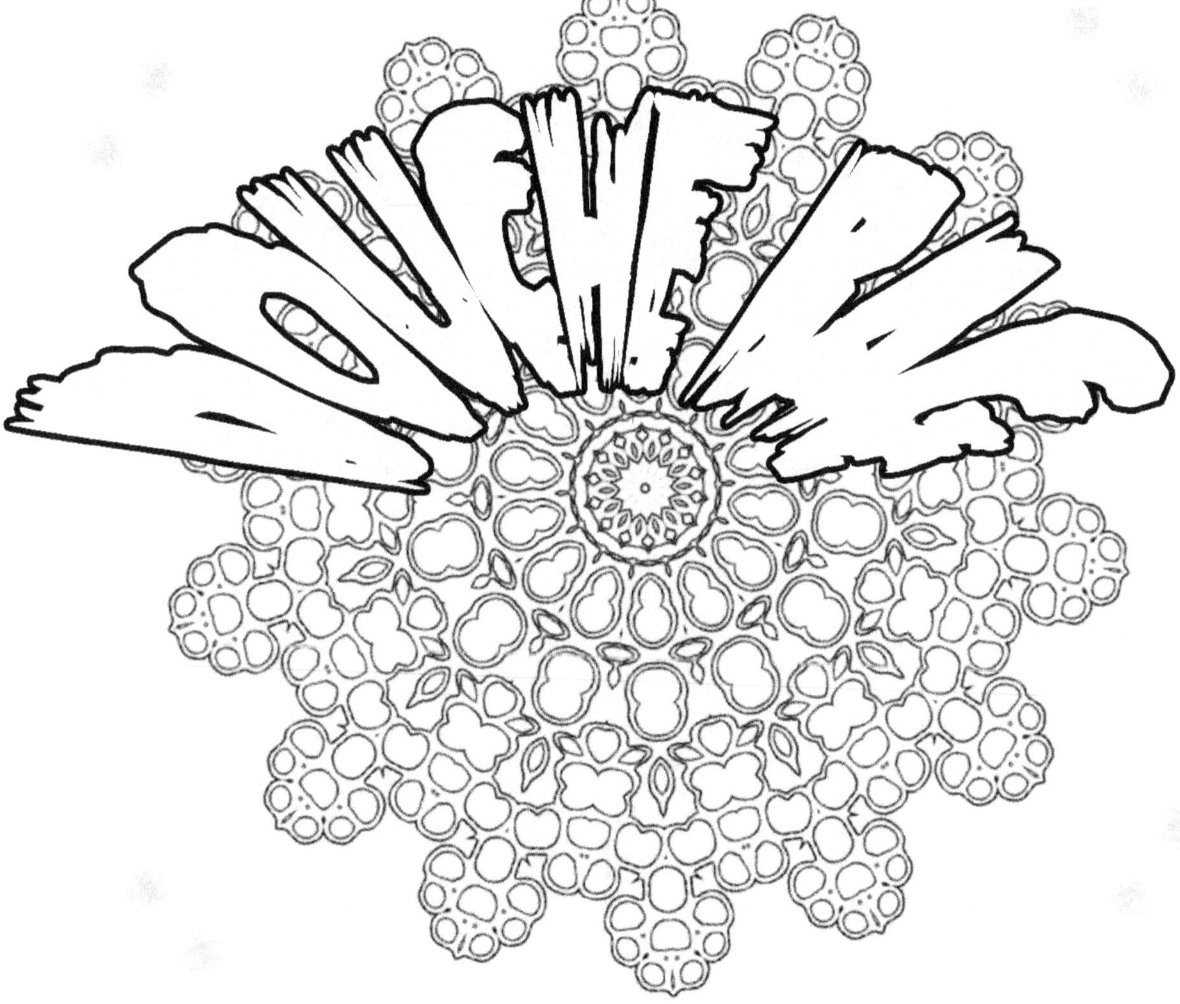

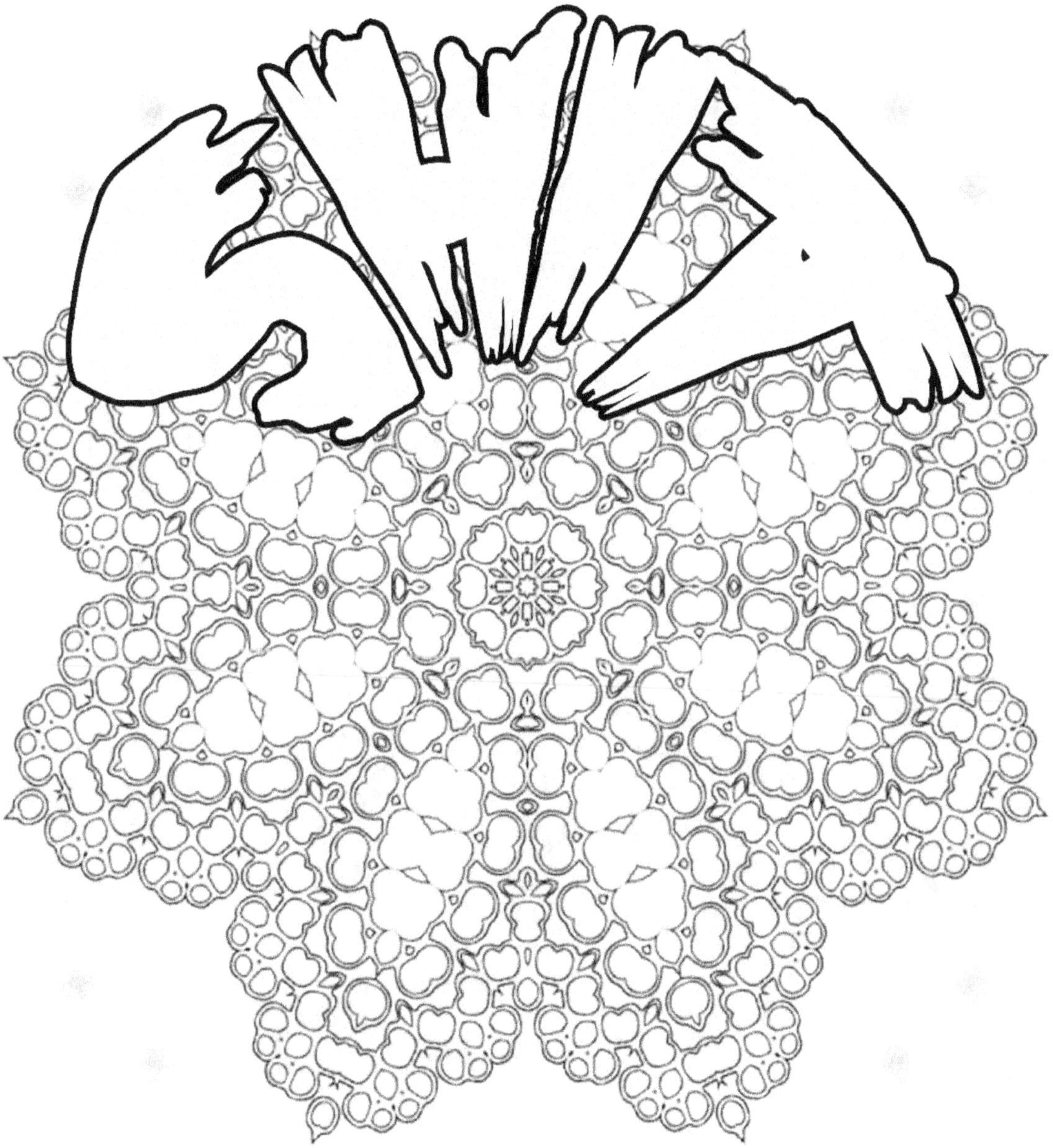

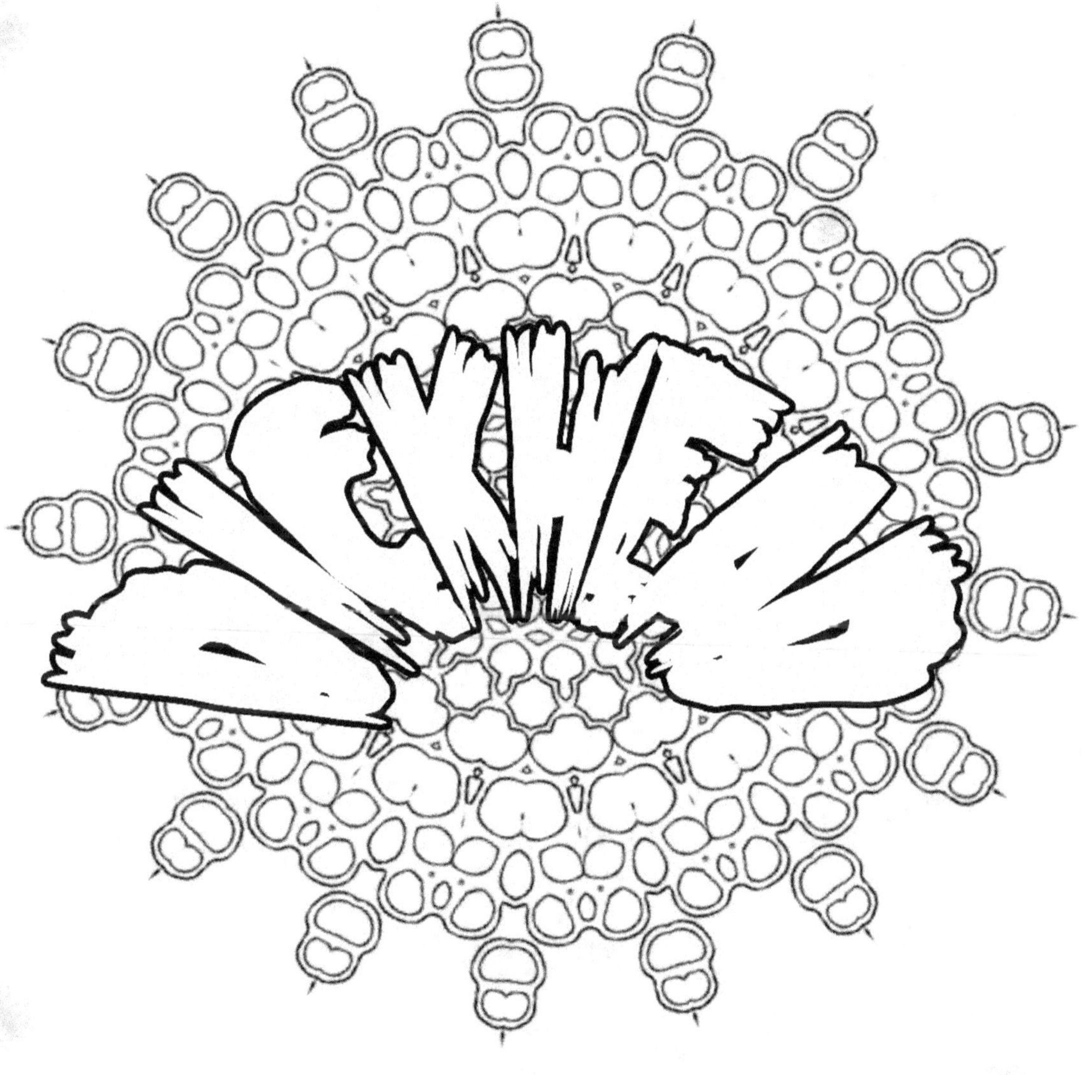

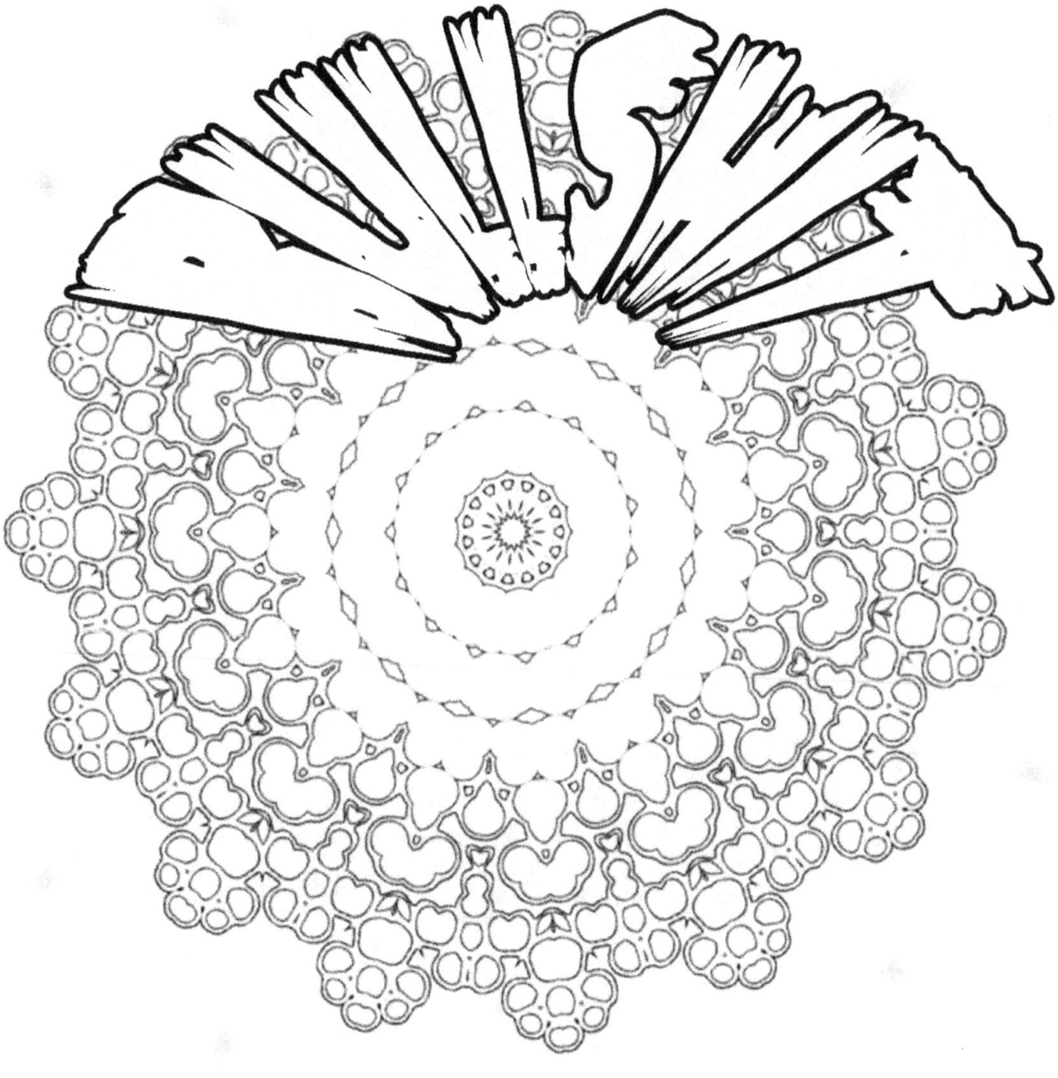

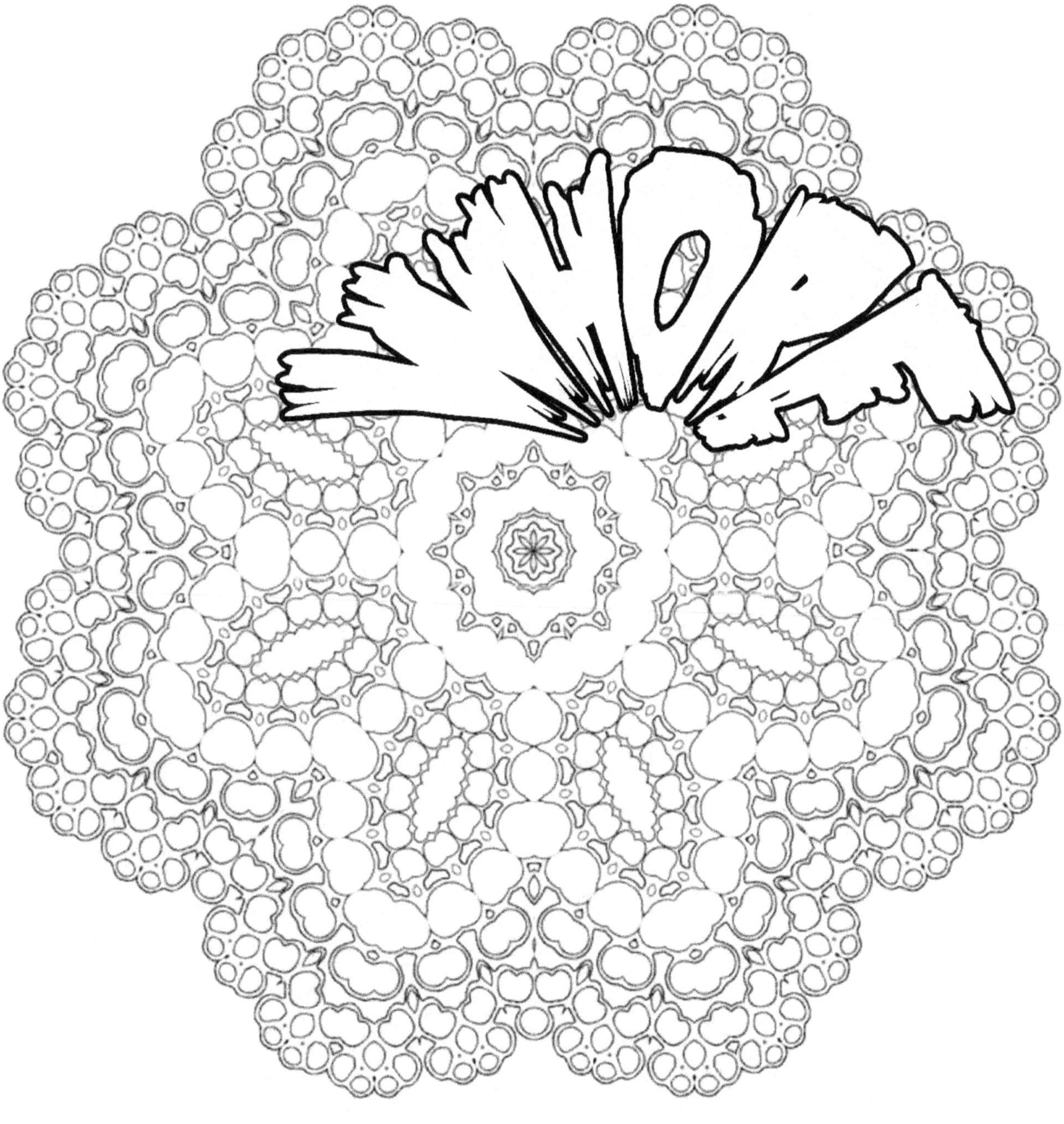
WHOA

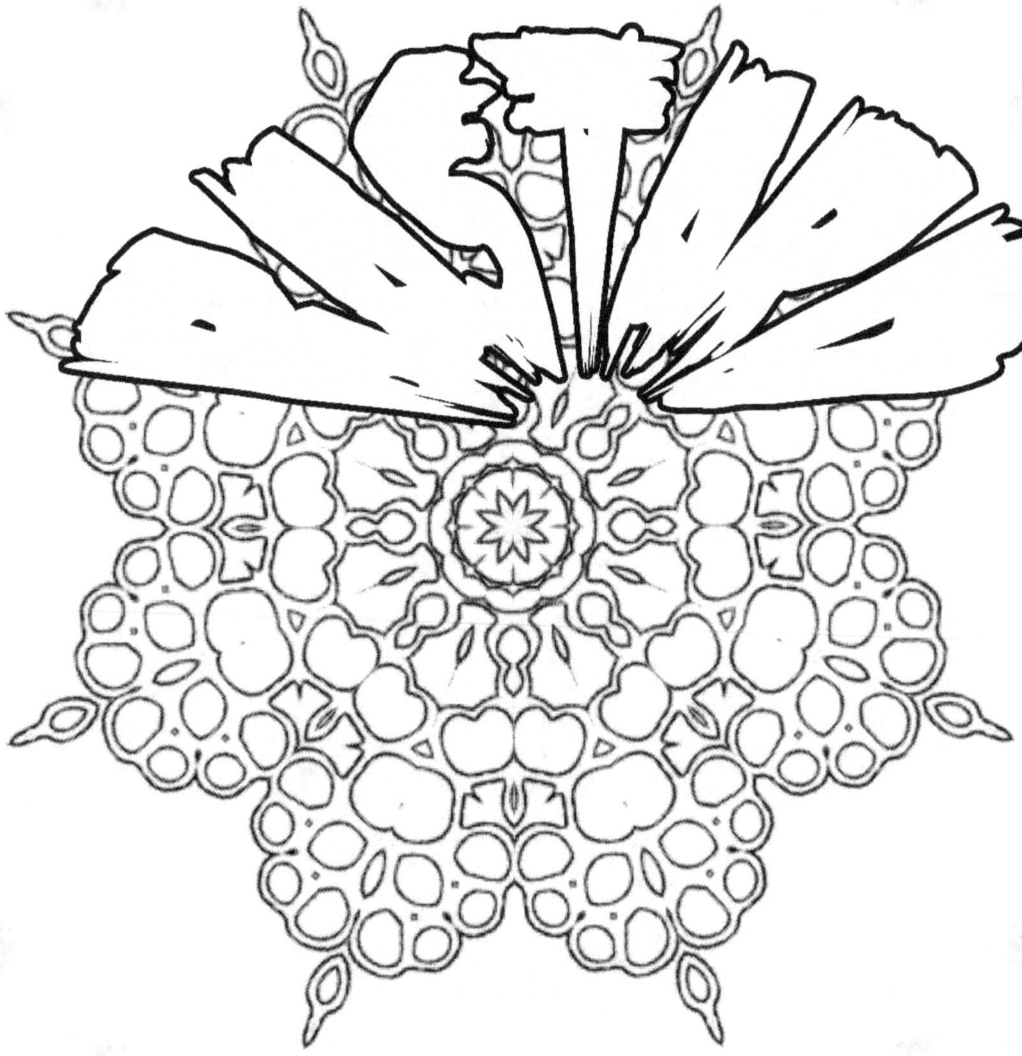

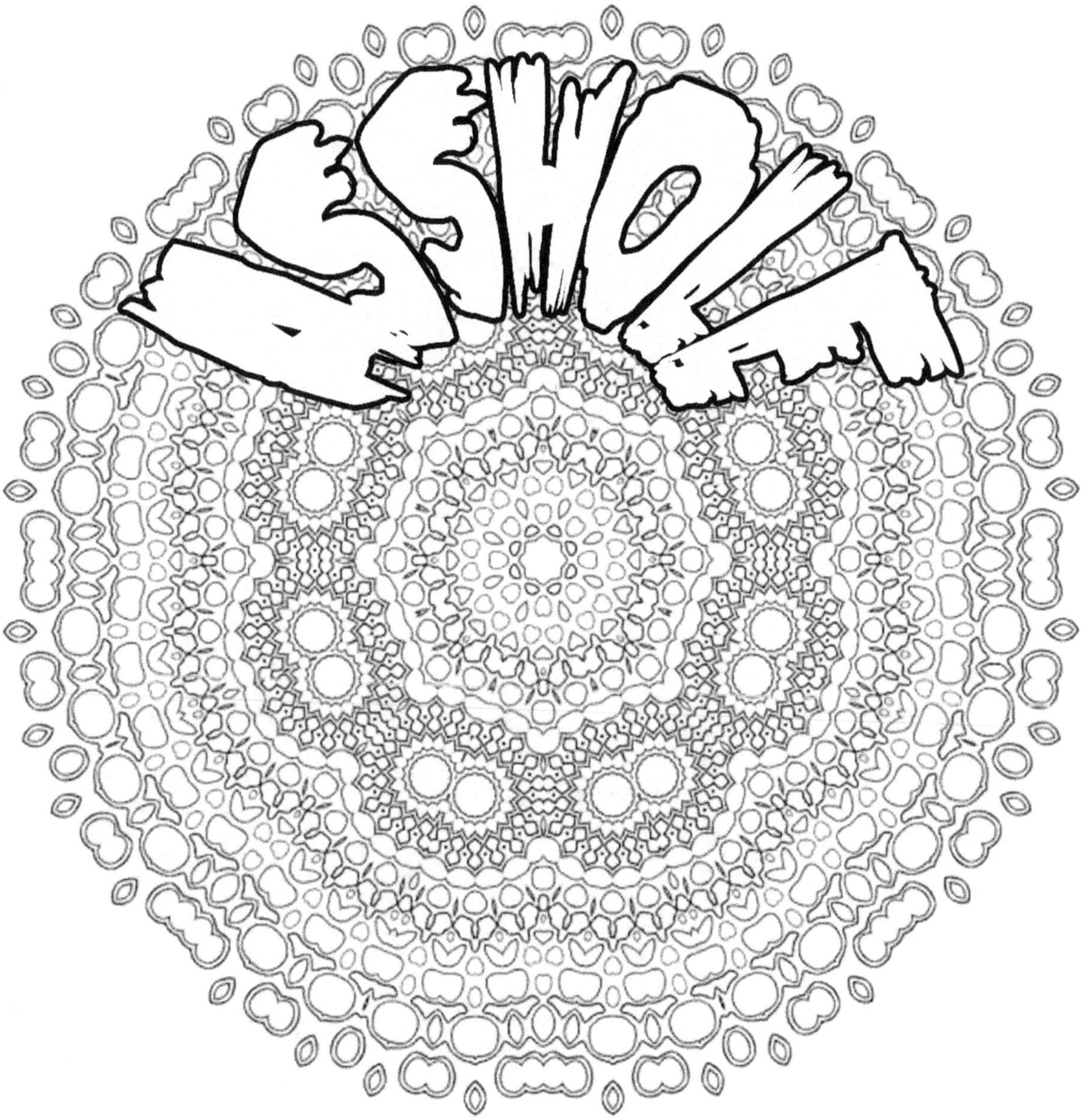

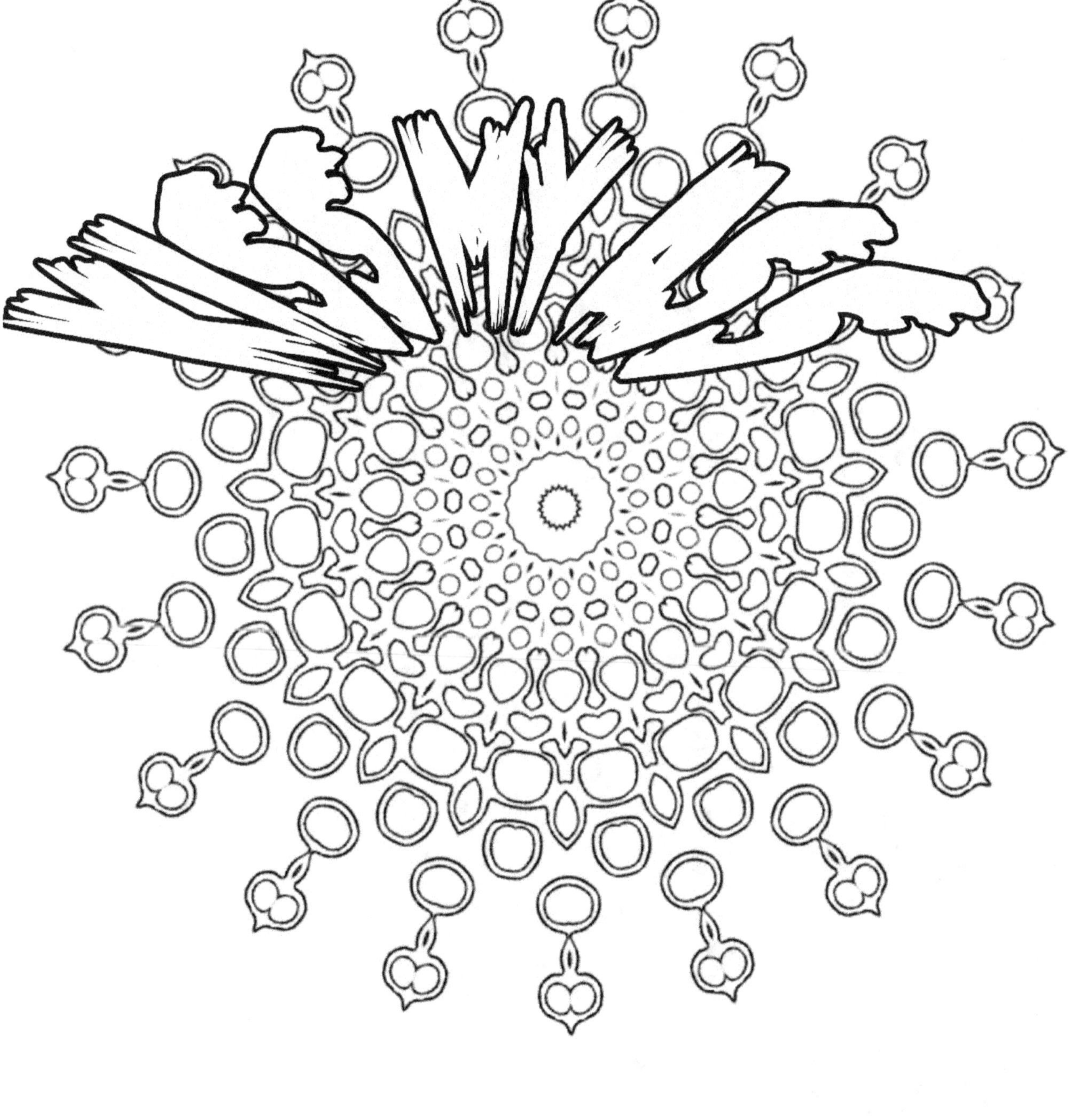

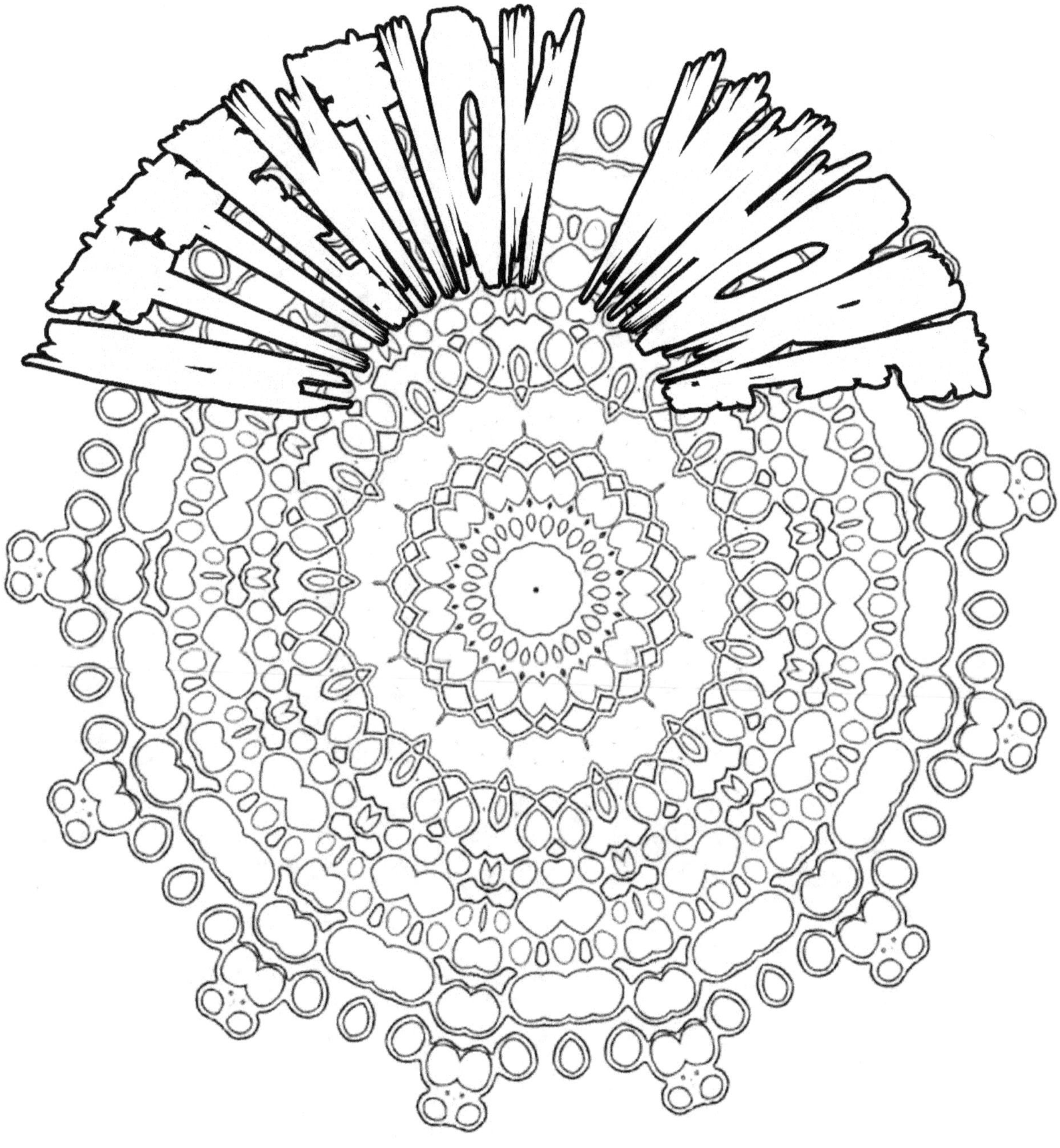

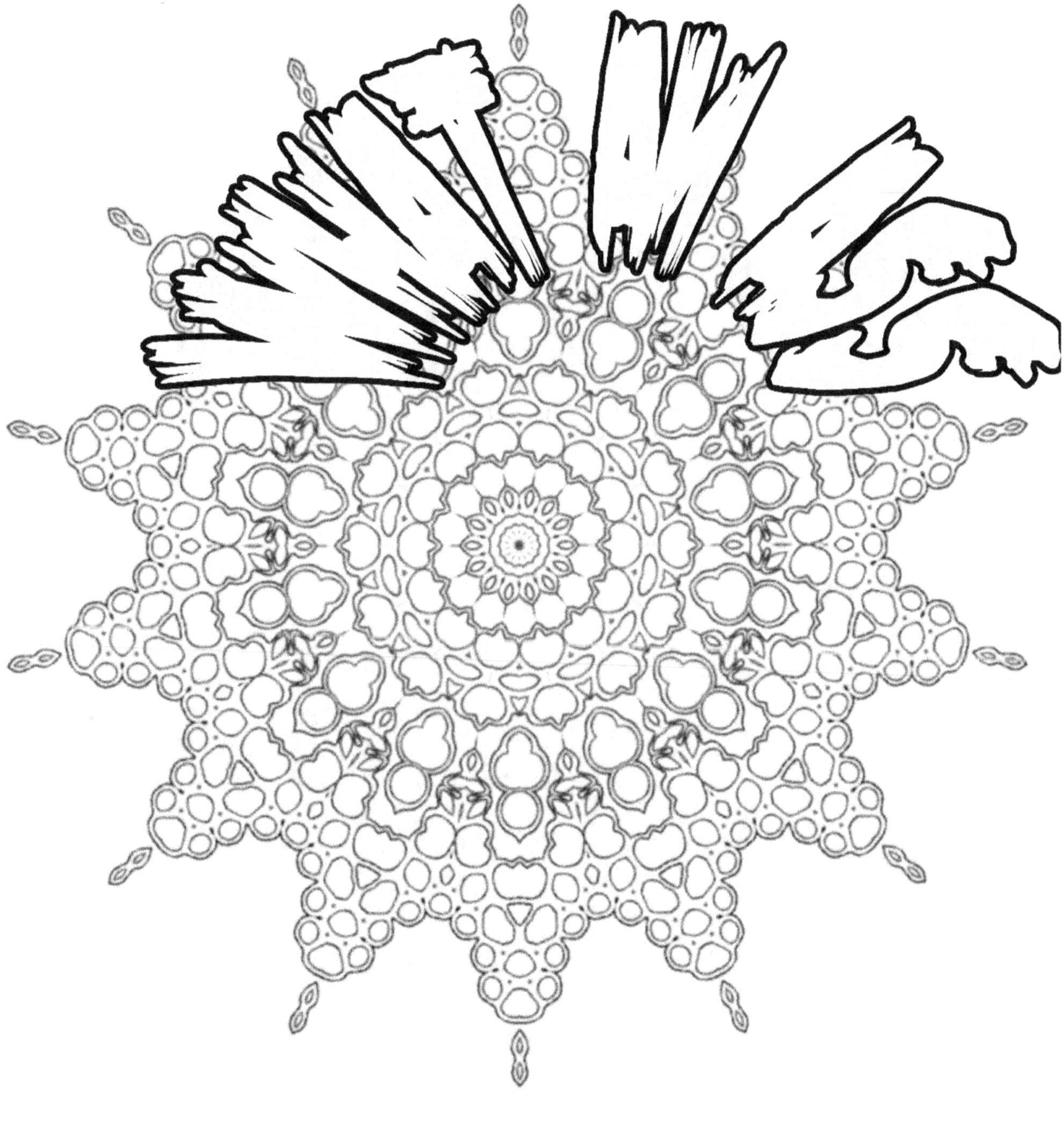

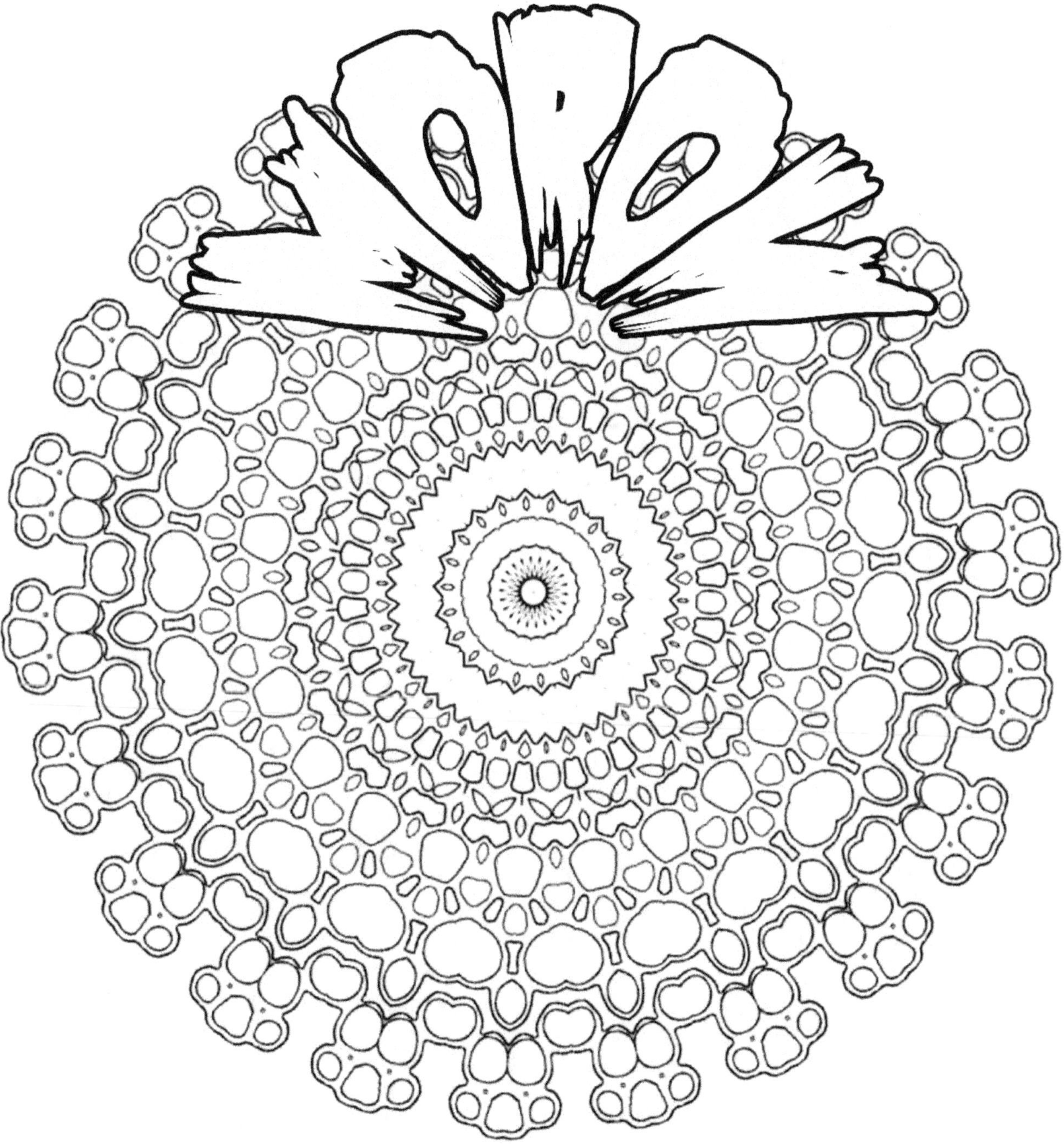

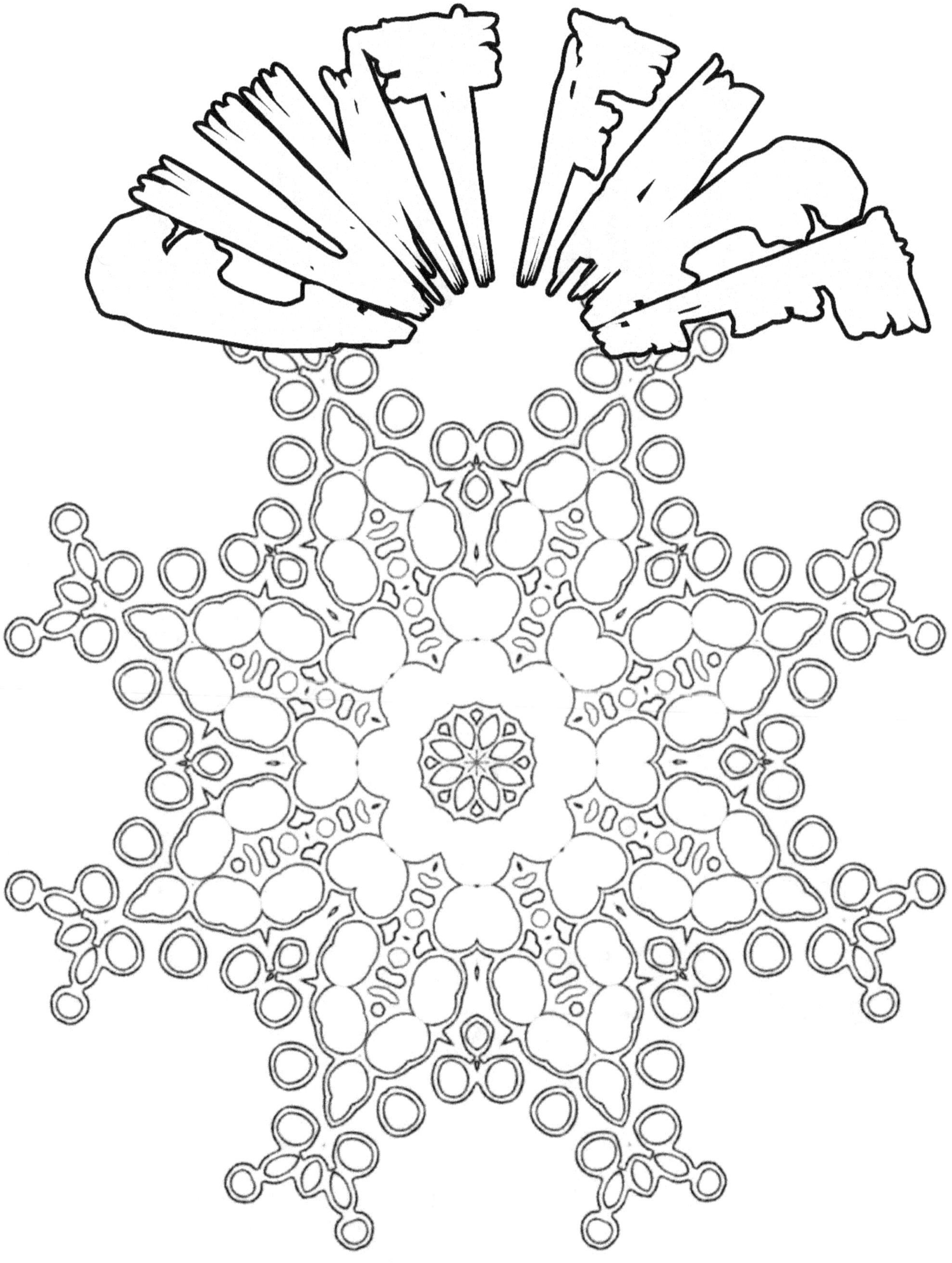

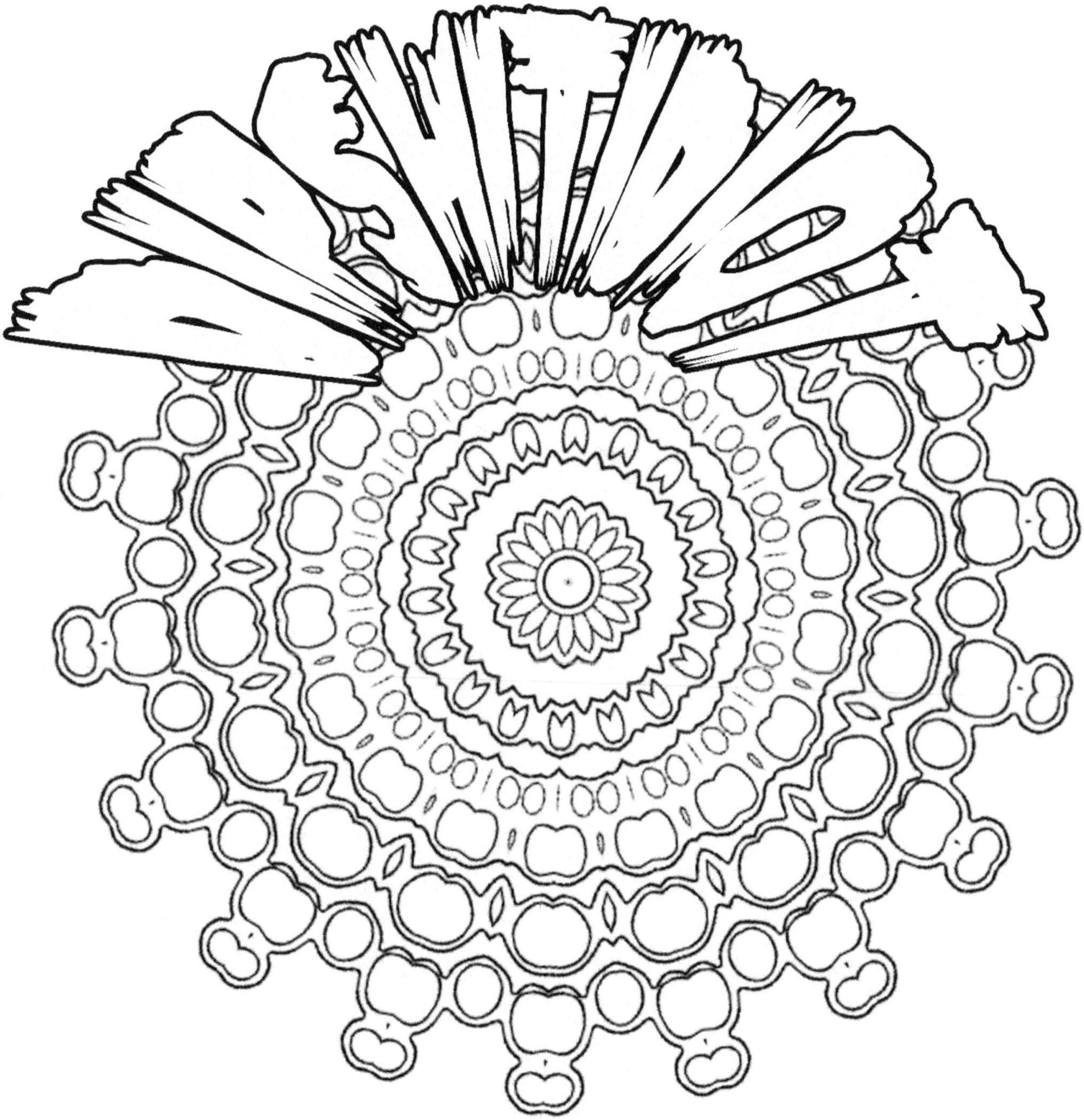

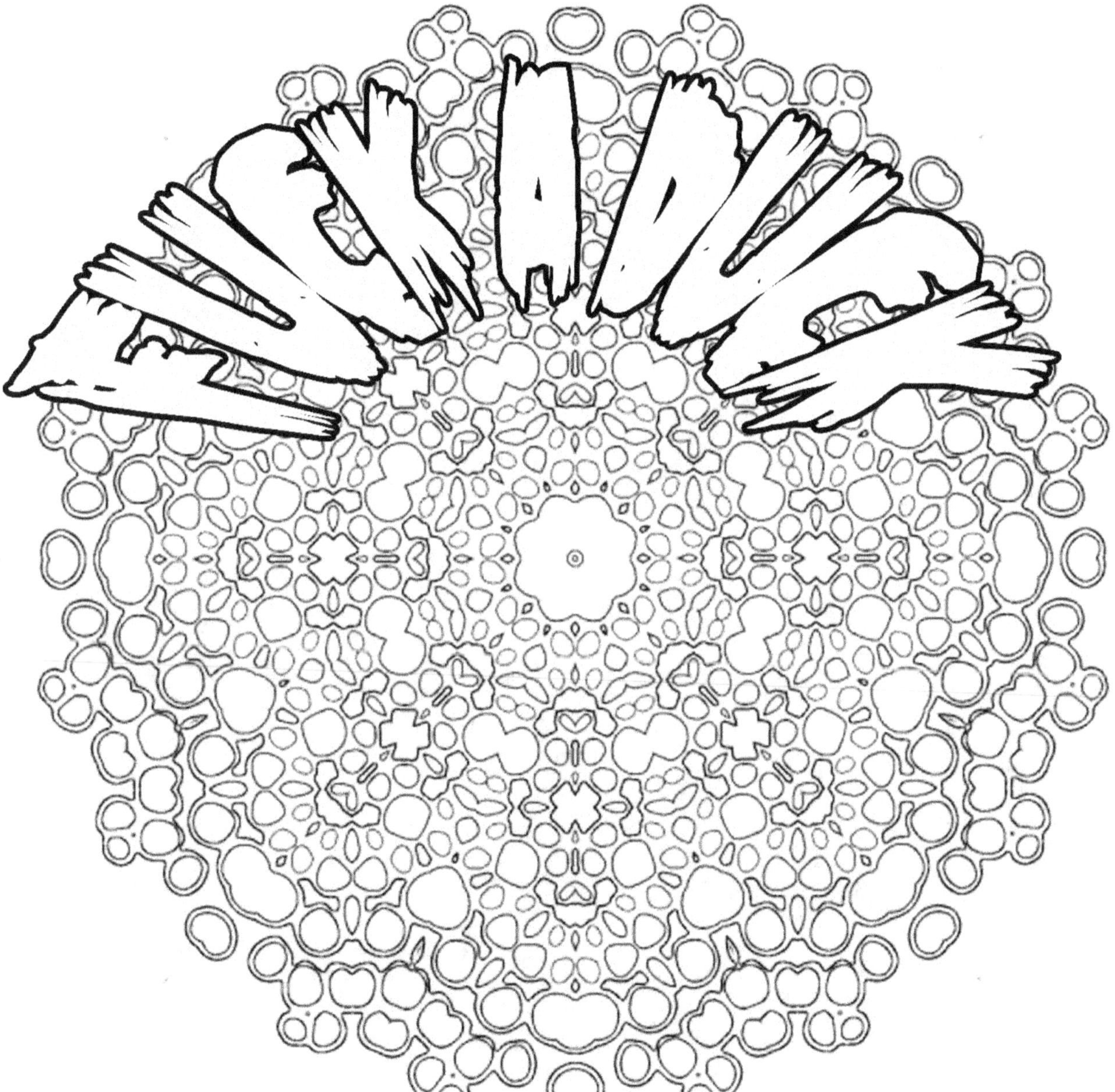

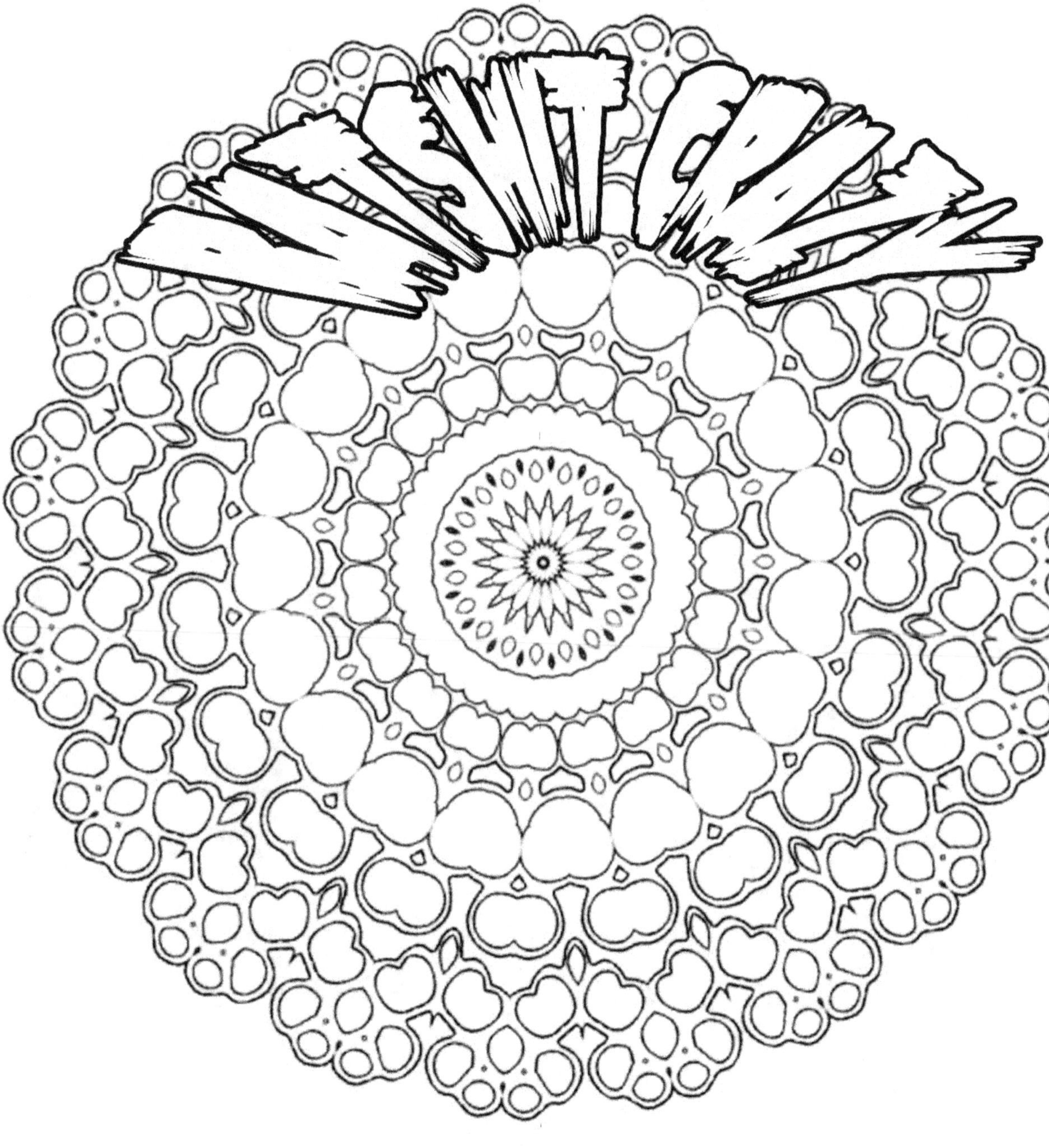

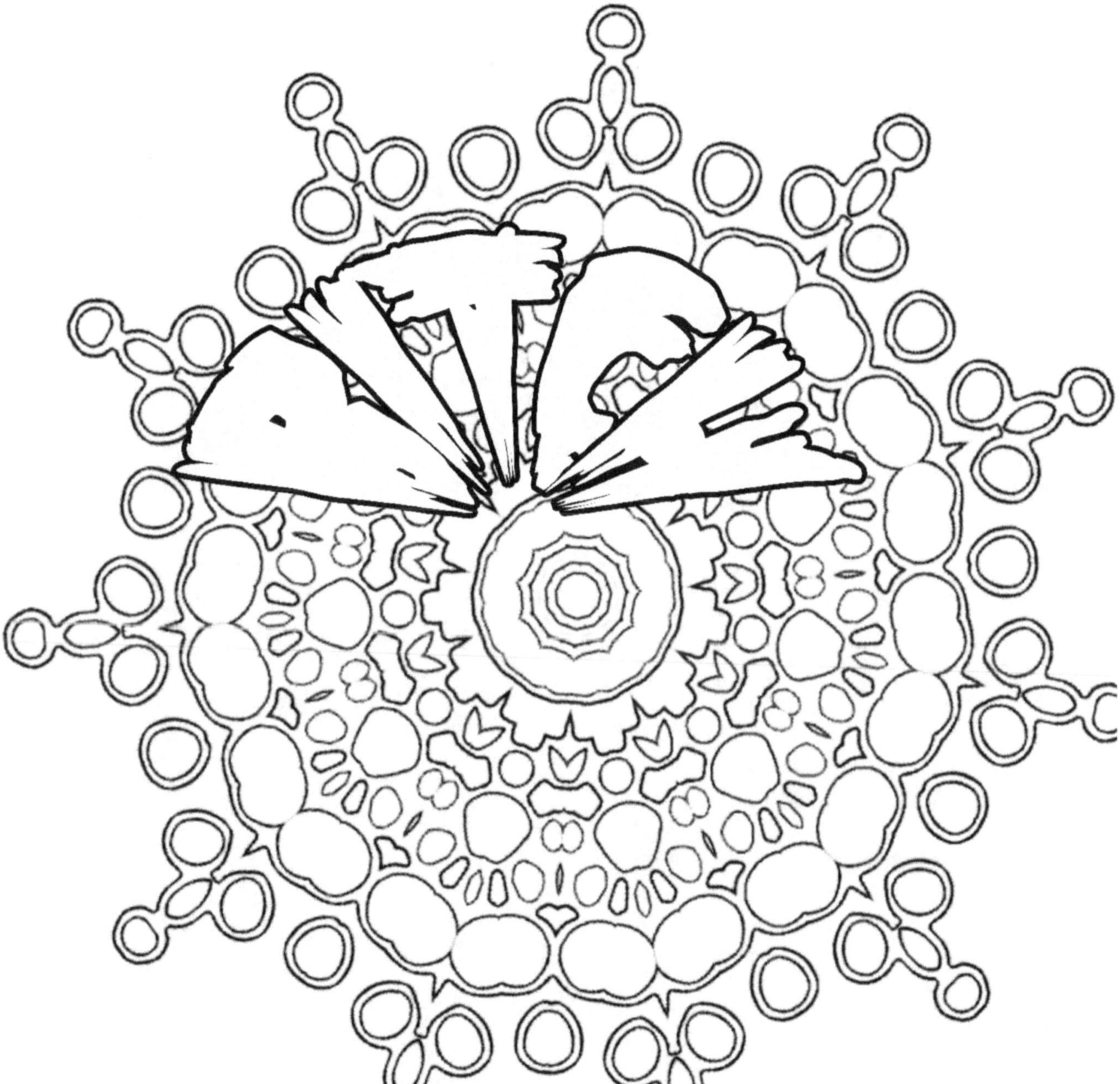

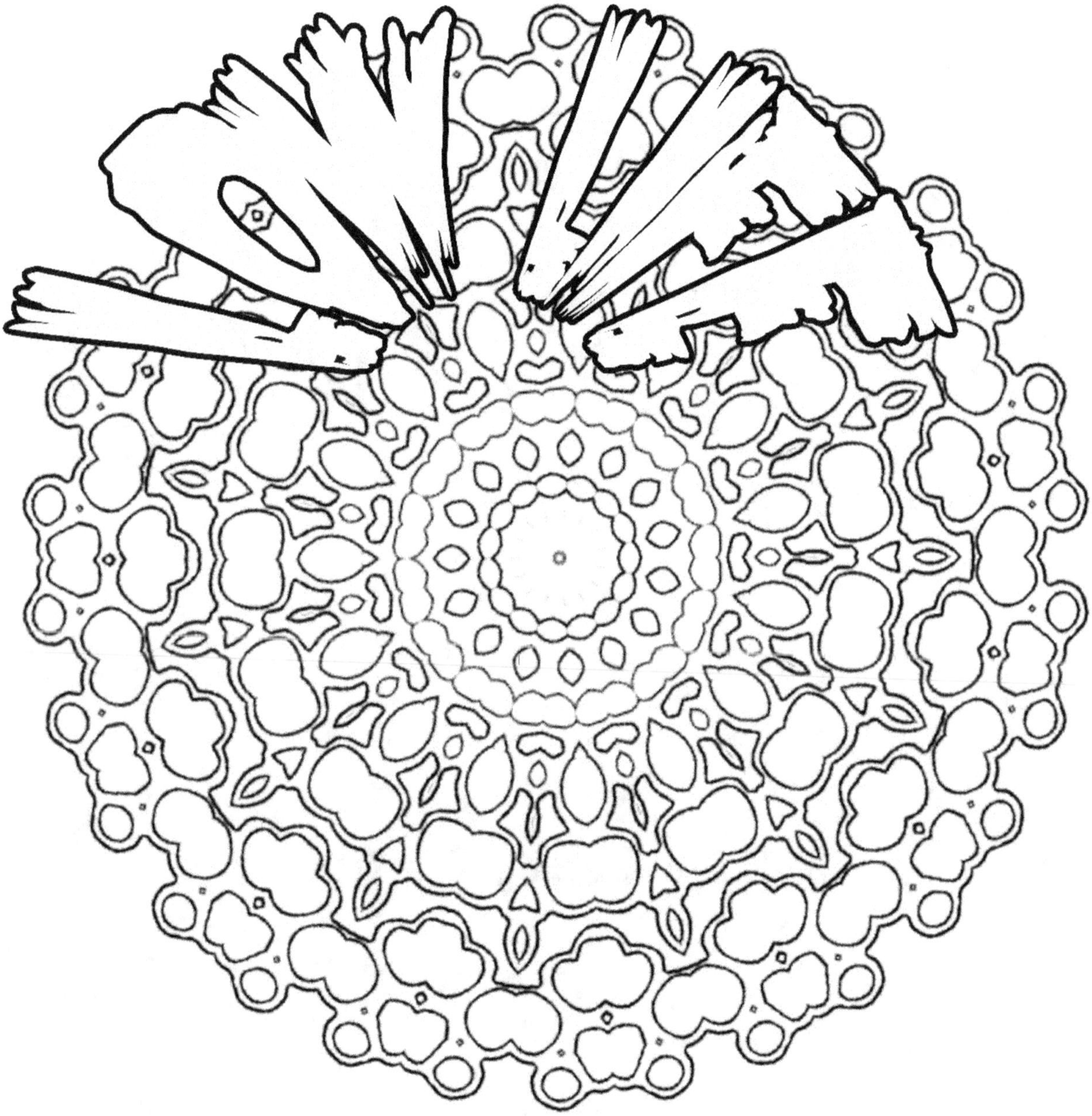

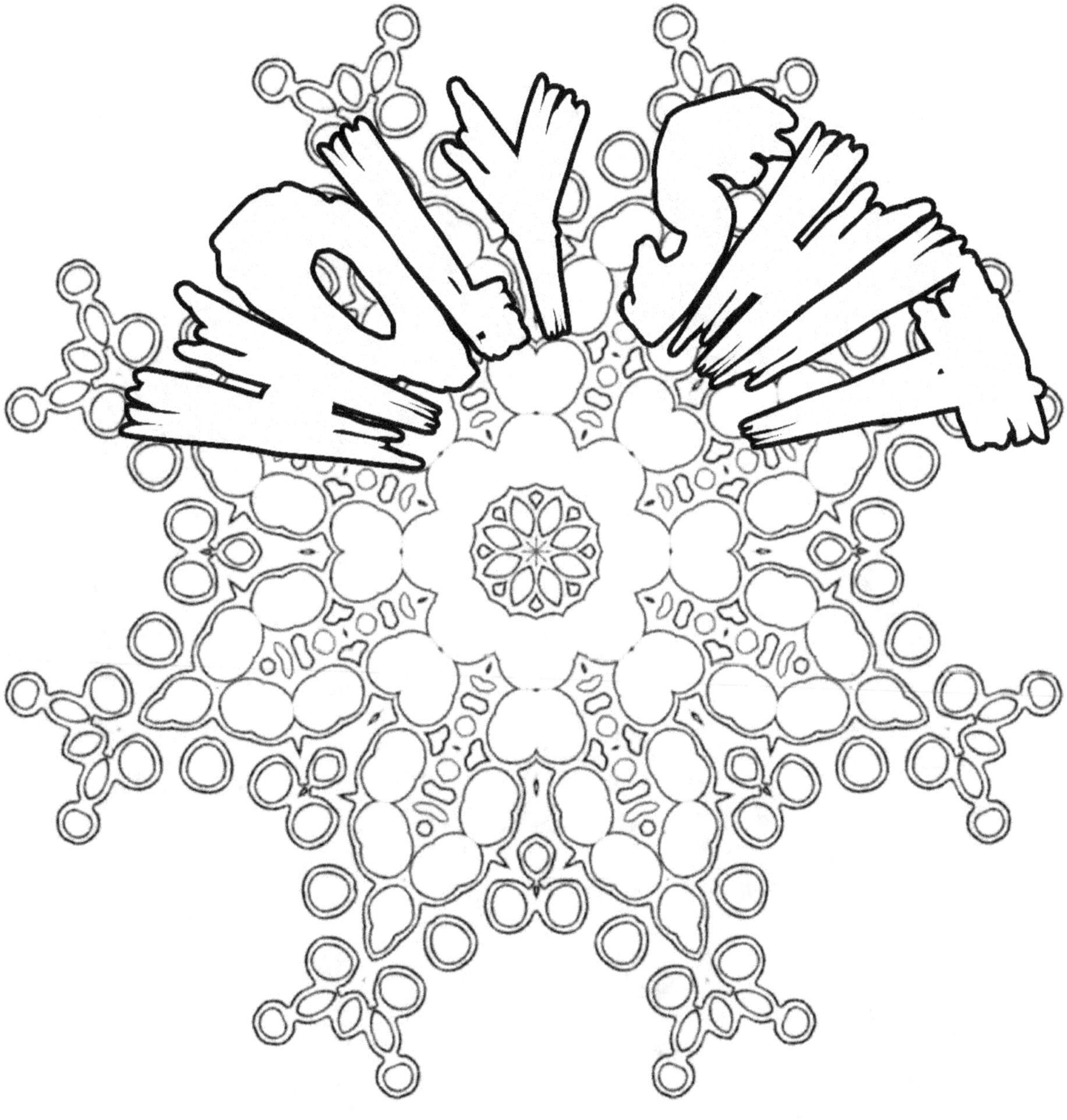
HOLY SHIT

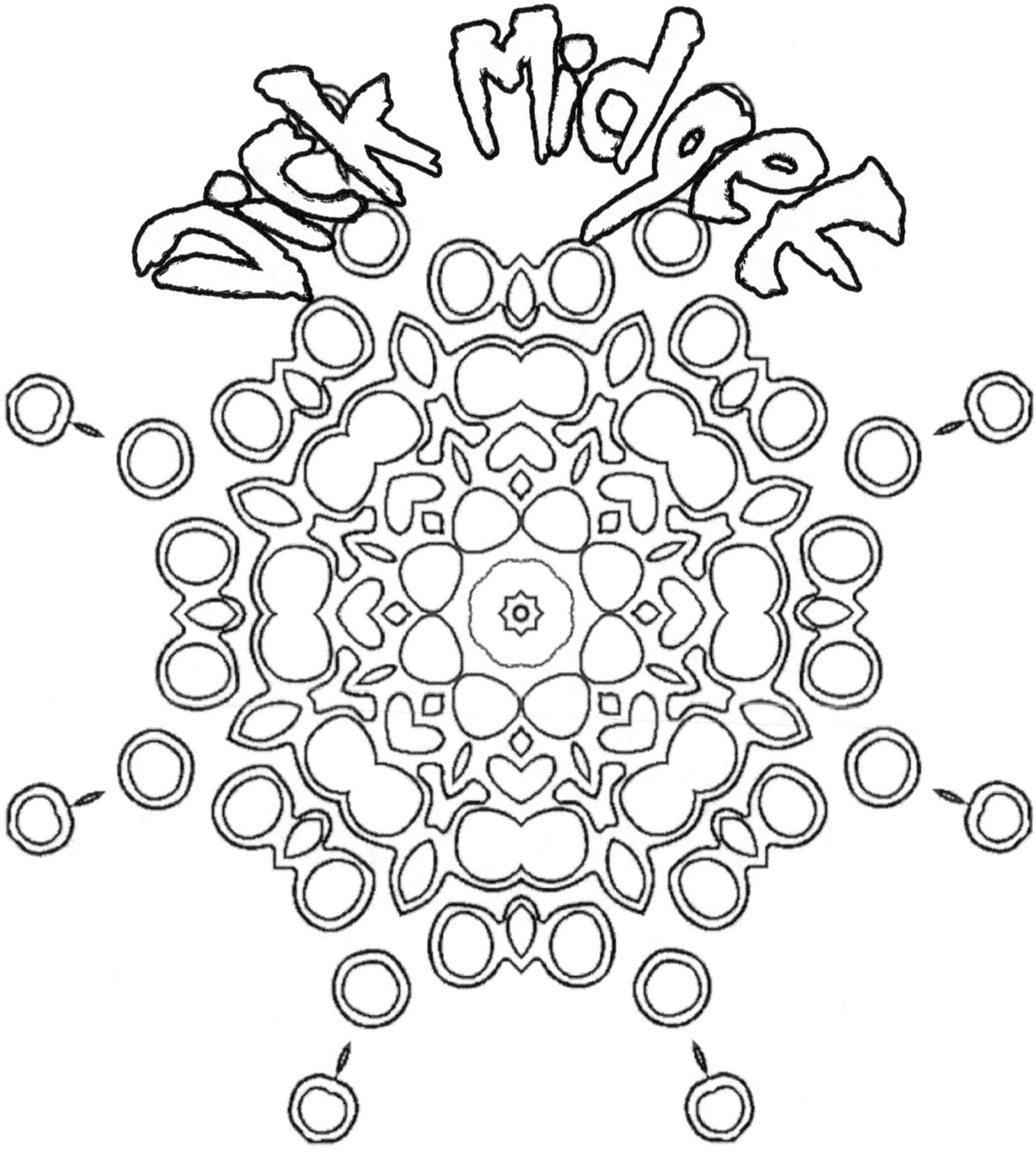
Dick Midget

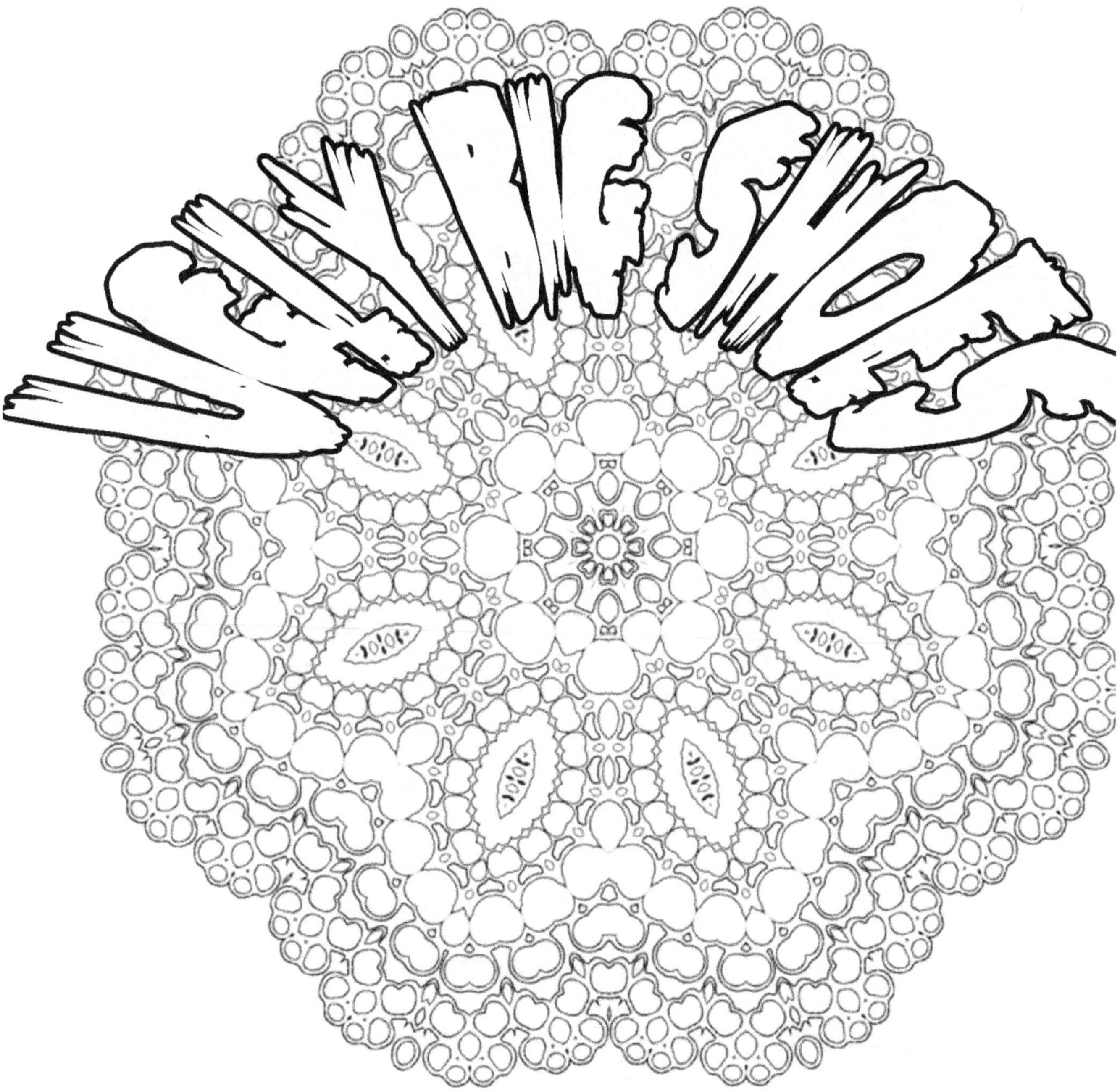
BIG SHOES

www.ingramcontent.com/pod-product-compliance
Lightning Source LLC
Chambersburg PA
CBHW081745170526
45167CB00009B/3934
* 9 7 8 1 5 4 4 0 6 2 0 2 0 *